Alexei's Week

by Antonia Barber

NATIONAL GEOGRAPHIC LEARNING | CENGAGE

It's Sunday at 3:00 a.m. Alexei can't sleep! He is worried about going to his new school.

It's Monday at 7:15 a.m. The bus is late.

SUNDAY	MONDAY	TUESDAY	WEDNESDAY	THURSDAY	FRIDAY	SATURDAY
⊗	1	2	3	4	5	6
8	9	10	11	12	13	

Mr. Clark is the bus driver.

Here is Alexei's homeroom.

It's 10:00 a.m. Alexei is lost.
Where is his homeroom?

It's Tuesday at 12:00 p.m. Alexei eats lunch.

Alexei sits by himself.

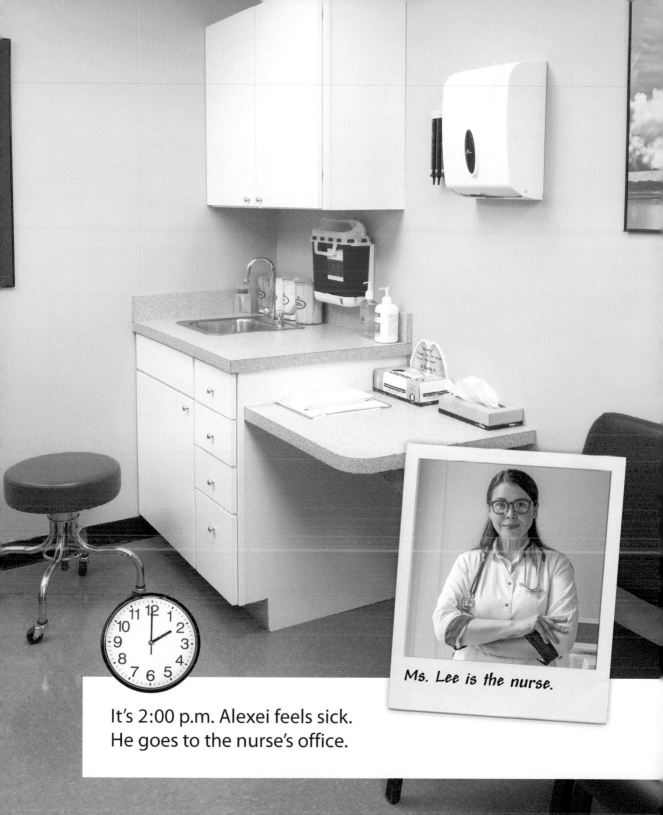

Ms. Lee is the nurse.

It's 2:00 p.m. Alexei feels sick.
He goes to the nurse's office.

It's Wednesday at 8:15 a.m.
Alexei is late for school. He goes
to the principal's office.

Mrs. Diaz is the principal.

It's 1:30 p.m. Alexei needs
a lab partner.

Yana is Alexei's new lab partner.
She is from Russia, too.

It's Thursday at 12:00 p.m. Alexei drops his lunch tray.

Hugo helps Alexei pick up his tray.

Hugo's mom drives
Alexei home.

It's 3:00 p.m.
Alexei misses the bus.

It's Friday. Alexei has a good day.

SATURDAY

6

13

20

He finds his classroom.

He eats lunch with friends.

He sits with Yana on the bus.

It's Saturday at 11:00 a.m. Alexei helps his dad in the yard.

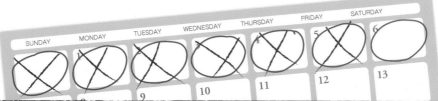

Alexei cuts the grass.

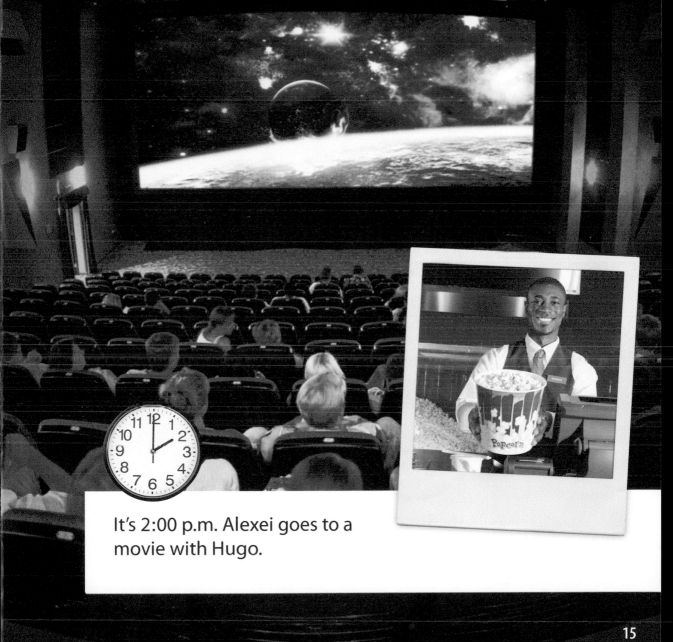

It's 2:00 p.m. Alexei goes to a movie with Hugo.

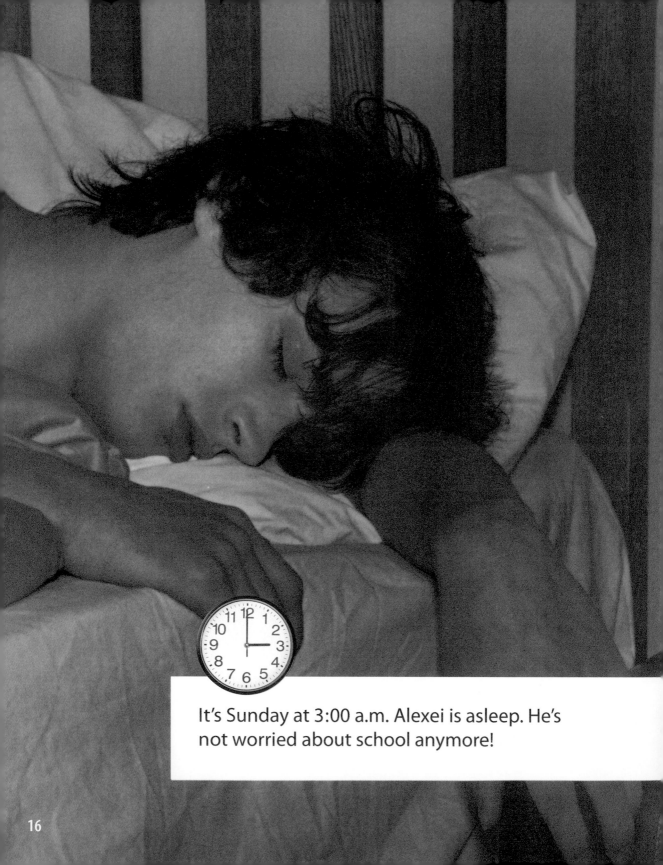

It's Sunday at 3:00 a.m. Alexei is asleep. He's not worried about school anymore!